IMPACT OF COVID-19 ON EDUCATION IN INDIA

VOLUME 2, ISSUE 1 OF BRAIN BOOSTER ARTICLES

SUSHMITHA J

Contents

Preface

"Start writing, no matter what. The water does not flow until the faucet is turned on".

-Louis L'Amour

Hundreds of students and professors are contributing their work to Brain Booster Articles, we are here to provide ample information about Law and Contemporary issues. Our aim is to provide a platform for today's generation to express their views and ideas on law and contemporary law.

Publication

This research paper is published in volume 2, issue 1 of Brain Booster Articles

Author

CHAPTER ONE

ABSTRACT

The spread of pandemic COVID-19 has drastically has thrown in great dilemma in every aspects of human life including education. It has significantly disrupted the education sector which is a critical factor of the future economy of our country. Educational institutions in India are based on based only on traditional method of learning which the conventional set is up of face to face lectures in a classroom. About 32 crore learners stopped to move to school or college and on all educational activities came to rest in india. Outbreak of COVID-19 has thought us a concept that change is inevitable.for coping up with the unpredictable situation the educational sector has been fighting to survive the crisis by adopting different approach and digitizing the challenges to crumble away the threat of pandemic.

This paper highlights some measures taken by government of India , the both positive and negative impacts of COVID-19 on education , various challenges and opportunities created by COVID-19 are discussed additionally some Post COVID-19 trends are outlined along with that some fruitful suggestions are also pointed.

Keynotes: Education, Online learning, Pandemic, Impacts, challenges, Post COVID-19.

CHAPTER TWO

METHODOLOGY

data and information present in this research paper are collected from various reports which are been prepared by national and international agencies on COVID-19, informations are collected from several authentic websites and journals relating to impacts of COVID-19 on educational system are referred.

CHAPTER THREE

INTRODUCTION

The COVID-19 pandamic has spread world wide and has notably disrupted the education sector. it has affected more than 4 million people all over the world. As per the UNESCO report during mid april 2020 more than 90% of total world student population have been affected by the pandemic which reduced slowly to 67% by june 2020. The outbreak of covid 19 has influenced more than 120 crore of student and youth across the world.

In india around 32 crore of students have been affected by numerous curtailment, restrictions and the nation wide lockdown for COVID-19. According to UNESCO report, primary students of 14 crores and 13 crores of secondary students are troubled and damaged, which are the two mostly affected level in India.

Noticing the corona virus pandemic situation the WHO advised to maintain social distancing as one of the first precautionary step in which every country started the action of lockdown to decrease the spread of virus influences. Focusing on educational sectors including schools, colleges and universities there was closure announced, they suspended the classes and all examinations including entrance test at school, college and university level were postponed. Every student most academic schedules were mostly pulled down by lockdown measures.

Lockdown has compelled many educational institutions to call off the direct classes, examinations, internships, extra-curricular activities etc, rather to choose and continue in online mode. However, it is an exceptional circumstance in the history of education, COVID-19 has designed various opportunities to come out of rigorous classroom teaching methods to a new era of digital model.

At the beginning, switching to this style of new learning was difficult and hard to cope up with the pandemic situation. Later on surviving was a vital task of every living in this world adopting changes to accept life and survive people shifted slowly to the new era of life concerning even in educational side. COVID-19 created many opportunities and challenges for educational institutes to strengthen their technological knowledge.

CHAPTER FOUR

OBJECTIVES

The present research paper focused on the following objectives:

- To enlighten various measures taken by government of India during pandemic on educational sector.
- To highlight various opportunities and challenges created on educational system by COVID-19.
- To highlight the both positive and negative impacts of COVID-19 on education.
- To enlist the Post COVID-19 trends of education and to put some effective suggestions for continuing education during pandemic situation.

CHAPTER FIVE

ONLINE EDUCATION

"ONLINE EDUCATION IS NO MORE AN OPTION RATHER IT IS NECESSITY"- lockdown has given many people a spark of hope in learning even in the most risky situation. Foe both teachers and students to continue their educational activities through online is a ray of hope on continuing our routine without sparing our lives. Many universities digitalized their operations in eduactional sector understanding the need of their current pandemic situations.

It was an overnight shift from normal classrooms into e-classrooms in which the educators have shifted their entire pedagogical approach to tackle the new advanced conditions and adhere to the changing situation. With the help of internet the method of learning should get adopted example: delivering lectures through video conference using different apps like zoom, google meet, webex, facebook, youtube, skype etc.

Numerous educational institutions in India are not furnished with digital facilities and also not every students is well equipped with high speed internet and advanced digital gadgets to cope up with the immediate change from traditional educational set up to online education system. Distance and personalized teaching and learning were the challenges by through innovative solutions it can help to wash away the trouble.

The google products helped to overcome the problematic situations example: gmail, google forms, google drive, google classroom, jam board and drawings, calenders, open board software etc are successful tools used as an alternative method for face to face normal classes.

CHAPTER SIX

PROBLEMS FACED IN ONLINE LEARNING

Modern technological range from downloading errors, issues with installation, login troubles, problem with audio- video, personal attention is also huge issue faced by online classes.

Students felt lack of communication, technical problems and difficulty in understanding . in a report half of the students found difficulties in balancing their education on one hand with other works, family and social lives on the other. Many students were also found to be inadequately prepared for several academic and e-learning competencies.

In this hard time, the entire concern is not about quality of education provided through this online education to the students, it is preferable the action took on the crisis . having few amount of knowledge in a very hectic situation and having 0 % knowledge in that risky and hectic situation is totally different. We were in need to adopt and adhere to changing conditions following our routine without sparing our lives is highly important.

CHAPTER SEVEN

INITIATIVES TAKEN BY GOVERNMENT OF INDIA ON EDUCATION DURING COVID-19

Nearly all state government ministries have taken measures to make sure that academic activities in schools, college, universities do not restrain or get restricted during the lockdown period.

The brought a safety line step "online" learning, instructed all schools and colleges and other educational sector to hold on online classes. Online learning was the only best solution which can be implemented during the pandemic COVID-19 situation.

Ministry of Human Resource Development (MHRD) brought many arrangements including online portals and educational channels through direct door step of home, TV, radio for all level students to continue learning.

- Diksha portal: it contains e-Learning content for students, teachers, and parents aligned to the curriculum, including video lessons, worksheets, textbooks and assessments. Under the guidance of its national boards of education (CBSE) and NCERT, the content has been created by more than 250 teachers who teach in multiple languages. The app is available to use offline. It has more than 80,000 e-Books for classes 1 to 12 created by CBSE, NCERT in multiple languages. The contents can also be viewed through QR codes on textbooks. The app can be downloaded from IOS and Google Play

- e-Pathshala: it is an e-Learning app by NCERT for classes 1 to 12 in multiple languages. The app houses books, videos, audio, etc. aimed at students, educators and parents in multiple languages including Hindi, Urdu, and English. In this web portal NCERT has deployed 1886 audios, 2000 videos, 696 e-Books and 504 Flip Books for classes 1 to 12 in different languages. Mobile Apps is available.
- National Repository of Open Educational Resources (NROER) portal: it provides a host of resources for students and teachers in multiple languages including books, interactive modules and videos including a host of STEM-based games. Content is mapped to the curriculum for classes 1-12, including aligned resources for teachers. It has a total of 14527 files including 401 collections, 2779 documents, 1345 interactive, 1664 audios, 2586 images and 6153 videos on different languages.

2. Higher Education:

Swayam is the national online education platform hosting 1900 courses covering both school

- Swayam: it is the national online education platform hosting 1900 courses both school (classes 9 to 12) and higher education (under graduate, post graduate programs) in all subjects including engineering, humanities and social sciences, law and management courses. The unique

feature is that, it is integrated with the conventional education. Credit transfers are possible for SWAYAM courses.

- Swayam Prabha has 32 DTH TV channels transmitting educational contents on 24 x 7 basis. These channels are available for viewing all across the country using DD Free Dish Set Top Box and Antenna. The channel schedule and other details are available in the portal. The channels cover both school education (classes 9 to 12) and higher education (undergraduate, postgraduate, engineering Out-of-school children, vocational courses and teacher training) in arts, science, commerce, performing arts, social sciences and humanities subjects, engineering, technology, law, medicine, agriculture.
- e-PG Pathshala is for postgraduate students. Postgraduate students can access this platform for e- books, online courses and study materials

during this lockdown period. The importance of this platform is that students can access these facilities without having internet for the whole day.

CHAPTER EIGHT

POSITIVE IMPACTS

Educational institutions in India have accepted and adopted the changes and trying to make use of the best provided for the students during this COVID-19 pandemic. The Indian educational system has got opportunities for transformation from traditional system to a advanced new era

- Rise of learning management: there are greater opportunities available for mainly developing and strengthening the learning management system is opened.
- World wide exposure: there are opportunities to interact with peers all over the world for the learners and educators as well.
- Blended learning: COVID-19 has accelerated adoption of digital technologies to deliver education. Assessment of learning had showed immense opportunities for major transformation in area of curriculum development and pedagogy.
- Large learners: access to large pools of learners at one time.
- Open and distance learning: ODL encourages self-learning by providing various opportunities to customized learning as per their need.
- Improved use of electronic media for sharing information: students canm easily share materials and clarify doubts and queries related to it and resolve through easy access of email, SMS, phone calls and by using different social Medias like whatsapp etc.
- Enhance use of soft copy: soft-copies are easy for sharing and collecting materials can we used and shared for reference.
- Better time management: effectively and efficiently online education can be used as time saving and flexible.
- Rise in online meetings: there can be seen massive rise in telecommunication, virtual meetings, webinars and e- conferencing opportunities.

- Enhanced digital literacy: inducing use of digital technologies results in increasing digital literacy.

CHAPTER NINE

NEGATIVE IMPACT

Education sector has suffered a lot due to the outbreak of COVID-19. As coin has both sides the other side of impact on covid on education and some of them are as pointed below:

- Educational activity hampered: Classes have been suspended and exams at different levels postponed. Different boards have already postponed the annual examinations and entrance tests. Admission process got delayed. Due to continuity in lockdown, student suffered much difficulty in resuming schooling again after a huge gap.
- Impact on employment: Most of the recruitment got postponed due to COVID-19 Placements for students was also affected. In India, there is no recruitment in Govt. sector and fresh graduates fear withdrawal of their job offers from private sectors because of the present covidsituationsituation. The Centre for Monitoring Indian Economy's estimates on unemployment shot up from 8.4% inmid-March to 23% in early April and the urban unemployment rate to 30.9% When the unemployment increases then the education gradually decreases as people struggle for food rather than education.

- Unprepared teachers or students for online education- Not all teachers/ students are good at it or at least not all of them were ready for this sudden transition from face to face learning to online learning. Most of the teachers are just conducting lectures on video platforms which may not be real online learning without any dedicated online learning platform.
- Increased responsibility of parents to educate their wards: Some educated parents are able to guide but some may not have the adequate level of education needed to teach children in the house.

- Loss of nutrition due to school closure: Mid day meals is a school meal programme of the Government of India which is designed to provide better the nutritional food to school-aged children nationwide. The closure of schools has serious implications on the daily nutrition of students as the mid-day meal schemes have temporarily been shut. Various studies have pointed out that mid-day meals are also an important contributing factor for increased enrolment in the schools
- Access to digital world: As many students have limited or no internet access and many students may not be able to afford computer, laptop or supporting mobile phones in their homes, online teaching-learning may create a digital divide among students. The lockdown has hit the poor students very hard in India as most of them are unable to explore online learning according to various reports. Thus the online teaching-learning method during pandemic COVID-19 may enhance the gap between rich/ poor and urban/rural.
- Access to global education: The pandemic has significantly disrupted the higher education sector. A large number of Indian students who are enrolled in many Universities abroad, especially in worst affected countries are now leaving those countries and if the situation persists, in the long run, a there will be a significant decline in the demand for international higher education.
- Payment of Schools, Colleges fee got delayed: During this lockdown most of the parents will befacing the unemployment situation so they may not be able to pay the fee for that particular time periods which may affect the private institutes. integrated with a present-day mainstream higher education system.

CHAPTER TEN

POST COVID-19 TRENDS ON EDUCATION

- Improving in Personalized learning
- Students mobility may be reduced
- Social distancing in educational sector may continue
- Lack of Attendance
- Different shifts per day
- Artificial intelligence may be lead
- Open and distance learning may grow
- Debt crisis
- Unemployment rate is expected
- Not recognizing fresh graduates

CHAPTER ELEVEN

SUGGESTIONS

1. Develop creative strategies to ensure sustainable access to learning
2. Immediate measures to lessen the effect of pandemic on job opportunities, internship and research projects.
3. At present, requirement of technology and interest is must so, digital capabilities much reach to remotest and poorest to facilitate students to continue learning.
4. Public funds can be increased to fix internet gap.
5. As scientific innovations, values and benefits can be used to develop sustainable technologies and medicines it must be integrated with knowledge to access in educational system.
6. Safe and sound environment, proper safety measures and adequate quantity and quality learning in any mode to be provided.

CHAPTER TWELVE

CONCLUSION

Education sector has faced immense impact of COVID-19, government of India has taken many fruitful measures to meet those challenges. Our government has brought numerous opportunities simultaneously to survive and learn in this hard days. As, our nation is not completely equipped to reach all corners of education digitally, less privileged students may face difficulties to current choice of digitalizing. But many universities and Government of our nation are relentlessly trying to come up with solutions to resolve the challenges and threat . developing sustainable access to learning as well as other safety, sound precautions together would bring a better and new start on education sector in India.

Printed by Libri Plureos GmbH in Hamburg, Germany